Our thoughts and words

Stefka Harp

National Library of Australia Cataloguing-in-Publication entry

Creator: Harp, Stefka, author.

Title: Our thoughts and words/Stefka Harp.

ISBN: 9780992304096 (paperback).

Subjects: Australian poetry — 21st century.

Affirmations

Published with the assistance of www.wordwrightediting.com.au

Images courtesy of clker.com and bigstockphotos.com.

www.stefkaharp.com

Contents

Acknowledgements

I wish to express my deep and sincere gratitude to my parents for teaching me the value of life — how to love and be happy as well as show kindness; and to my siblings, for being a part of my life.

My thanks, too, to the Australian Government for opening the door for me to migrate and become a permanent resident; to experience a different kind of life, culture and customs, which has been very enriching, enlightening and eye-opening. I am very grateful for the opportunity I have been given and guided to get to the point I am at.

Sincere gratitude to:

- my daughter for her patience and loving assistance in proofreading my work
- Gail, publishing advisor for the guidance given.

Dedication

Everything I write and have written so far is dedicated to my family and the divine within, which has guided me through life. At times my ignorance and oblivion to the facts revealed has led to strife and suffering. But these experiences have given me the much-needed fuel for my writings, and I hope they will help others. Life is like a jigsaw puzzle. Some things are meant to happen so that the pieces fit within that puzzle.

S.H.

Disclaimer: The author is expressing beliefs and views based on her life experience. There is no intention to offend anyone who has contrary views. The poems are fun to read and in the process can bring a positive and loving attitude.

Introduction

These poems are, as the title suggests, all about our thoughts and words.

I have come to believe that the energy released by our thoughts and words creates our future to a degree. Certain individuals or groups of people that we encounter along our life journey could have an influence on us to learn a lesson. It could be either a positive, enhancing our lives, or a negative, bringing pain and suffering. Either way, it's a life lesson that can and should guide us from future pitfalls.

Our thought and word energy is the creator, and can attract people or events for our desires to come through, or can leave a bad taste in the mouth if negative thought energy has been released.

By becoming aware of our thoughts and words, and deeds as well, and choosing wisely, we will be on our way to receiving the fruits of out labour — *we shall harvest what we have sown.*

While I was working on the manuscript, I was constantly becoming aware of the thoughts, words and deeds I had executed and released, unintentionally or otherwise. I began nullifying my thought energies, as well as sending back other people's energy thrown at me, if there was any — whether envy and jealousy, being judged or hated, ill wishing, slander and the like.

Then one night — on 5 November 2016 to be precise — I was woken from my sleep to experience something that is not easy to describe or explain, or to be believed for that matter. There was this energy force in the form of a gassy wiggle, as big as my body, thick, smoky gray and heavy-going, snaking over me. It was as cold as ice; it felt as though I was going to be frozen. It snaked from the tip of my toes over me into the wall, through it and travelled on in a matter of a moment. It felt as if I had a brush with death.

It was a spooky event, but it did not spook me. The minute it disappeared, the room became warm and pleasant and I felt some kind of lightness within. At the time I could not explain what it was, and after a while I went back to sleep. In the morning I remembered the experience, recorded it in my journal and didn't think much about it.

I went on with my daily life, but in the back of my mind there was this gnawing, asking what it was to be revealed to me. It was not until March 2017, with the manuscript already sent to be edited, that it dawned on me. It was the other people's energy thrown at me from way back, that I have being praying to go back to the senders endorsed with my blessings and universal love. The energy accumulated so much strength over the years, and of cause made my life topsy-turvy. On many occasions my life was endangered to the point of near death. I could only imagine what that energy was going to do when it reached the senders, unless they knew how to nullify it. This kind of energy knows where to go exactly and precisely, as though it is composed solely of a brain that is all knowing and mighty powerful. It does not discriminate, does what it is sent to do and to whom. It is the invisible power. Good or bad depends on the thought and word energies released by the individuals.

The realisation of what that wiggle was came about by remembering an incident I had way back, which I have included in my autobiography.

One evening Stefka and Briana had an argument. Briana was in her early teens. Stefka asked her to do something for her which she refused. Not only did she refuse, but she turned around and said something nasty, with such anger, and with that she went into her room. Stefka got so hurt, and from the bottom of her heart yelled after her, 'I wish you would die tonight.' Immediately, she caught herself and very quickly said, 'Oh, God, I take it back', and left it at that. At that time she did not know how to cancel any thoughts or words released from the mind. The moment she said 'I take it back', she saw small blue–gray transparent, gassy, wiggly things floating around the corner of the hallway arch, coming into the dining room, and all of them roosted under one of the chairs and became invisible. Stefka was intrigued about what they were, but since they became invisible, she thought it was another trick of the eye. She did not think any further, and continued busying herself with her knitting.

Soon she went to bed herself and fell asleep. She could not tell how long she had slept when she was woken up feeling ill, like she had never experienced before in her life. It felt like she was dying. She can't begin to describe the ill feelings she had. The whole of her body was aching, she was trembling, she had difficulties breathing — you name it, she was suffering from it, and yet there was no sign of any cause that she could pin-point.

She survived the night with difficulties. Years later, she came to know what those blue–gray wiggles were. It was her own energy that she had sent to her daughter that came back to her. It almost claimed her life because she took it back. At that time, she wasn't aware of how to nullify thought and word energy, or repenting for that matter.

Then she understood how karma works, how all thoughts, words and deeds turn into powerful energy, and can and would do a lot of damage if negative and destructive to the receiver, and sooner or later to the sender. Now she knows it is better to dwell on the positive and always cancel the negative thoughts immediately. We are only human, and all kinds of thoughts go through our minds. Becoming aware of her thoughts, Stefka became selective what thoughts to give out and which onse were to be nullified.

I could easily imagine how the life on our planet is going to be if everyone becomes aware of their thoughts, and selective of what kind of energy they are going to release. We will be living in a golden age, long forgotten. No wars and bickering, only love, happiness, health and prosperity.

Nowadays technology might make life easier, but the core principal of the holy/universe never changes. Thoughts and deeds are powerful energies. Powerful enough to make or break a person, nation or the whole planet. Now is the time to unite and save the planet and ourselves.

As I said in the introduction to my book *Gratitude*:

Isn't it better to dwell on the positive? Even if there is nothing happening we are benefiting in many ways. Less stress means less tension in the brain, the heart muscle is more relaxed, we tend to be more pleasant and lovable — a delightful person to be around, that's for sure. I know what kind of thoughts I would feed my brain with, and release what kind of energy. Do you?

Stefka Harp

Priceless to know
Overall, to be sure.
Selection of words to flow,
I pray with faith to glorify, I
Trust the holy will unify,
It is imminent to purify, by
Vowing to think positively and smile,
Ever so to be one with the Divine.

Saintly, I make statements
To reflect the sentiments,
Although not always so,
Transformation does show
Eventually before I know,
Merrily I go about
Eliminating the doubt, I
Nurture the positivity day in and day out,
Time and again I shine,
Sincerity shown, like a child.

Time and again if I may,
Honestly I can say, the
Only way to be alive is to
Unite with the Divine.
God grant me one day at a time,
Hour on hour to shine, it is
The time of my life,
Sweet and serene, on the count of five.

Care I take about my thoughts.
Repent I do, and take notes
Every time my thoughts are out of sorts, I
Aim to repair and restore,
Temptation of evil thoughts to cast ashore, never
Ever to come across anymore.

Devote myself to loving thoughts
Entirely, for the record,
Swiftly everything comes to the fore,
The fruits of my kind endeavour galore,
In no time, desire fulfilled for sure
Near and far, with all my heart
Yearning to do my part.

Loving thoughts and words
On my mind from here forward,
Vigorously leading onward,
Excitement is the reward.

Competence surges,
Rapidly emerges,
Ensuring I don't go under,
Averting my blunder,
Tragic moment to divert,
Evidence to be on the alert,
Stumbling block to avert.

Expressing love and loving thoughts, I
Xero within to find God,
Confident I am no doubt
In the Divine I can count.
Tender loving care is found
Each time I send out
Many blessings through a prayer,
Embracing the world with care,
Nifty way with all my heart
To know truth in delight.

Existence only for the sake of it,
XYZ, is not enough for me.
Consciously I have to thrive, to
Instantly feel alive,
Therefore for me it's wise to
Elevate my soul and chime a
Melody that will reach the Divine, its
Excellence, loving and kind,
Now and eternally wants me to shine,
Today and forever more to be on my mind.

Blessed I am, excitement to find,
Radiance of love is a sign that
Inside of me is a Divine Child,
Never to resign from the Divine,
Graciously waiting to inspire,
Soul Divine to acquire.

Hallelujah, excitement everywhere!
Apparent here and there,
Permeating high and low,
Pertinently, to the point of a glow,
Invigorating my innermost self,
Non-stop to dwell,
Evoking passion above all.
Sheer joy for the soul,
Serenity and happiness are my goals.

Haven is the home for the soul,
Adequate for me to reach that goal,
Passionately with all my heart,
Paramount that I play my part,
Important it is to start, and
Not fall apart.
Elements of happiness give me a
Sense of wellbeing and harmony,
Soothing my soul as a balmy tea.

Inclined I am to feel confident
Now I am determined,
Selfishly I give myself a compliment.
There is love apparent,
Intensifying happiness at will,
Lovingly bringing peace to thrill,
Loving thoughts to overspill,
Serenity to know for the mind to instill.

Pacifies my step at best,
Encourages me to slow down and rest,
Ample loving thoughts I caress,
Comfort for the soul on a quest,
Eternal peace to find, and success.

Another day passing by with delight.
Nothing to worry about, but to invite
Devotion to the holy to ignite.

Hesitation is not in view,
As it is I start anew,
Rain or shine I go through.
Merriment I find, it is true,
Overjoyed I am without argue,
Non-stop to review, the
Everlasting love Divine to pursue,
Yearning for peace and harmony too.

It is in my interest to be

Consistent with my thoughts, you see,
Opposing destructive ones is the key,
Nullify them I do, on the count of three.
This is what I have come to know.
Intentionally I change for sure,
Night and day, I reassess and spiritually grow
Unfolding my true self to the core.
Overall, heart and soul ablaze,
Unfailingly I praise,
Softly, I sing and dance at a pace,
Lovingly I continue to pray,
Yielding peace all the way.

Responsible and wise indeed,
Essential to proceed,
Among all I decree,
Selfishly I agree,
Sheer joy it conveys,
Encouragement to pray and praise,
Saintly and truthfully always,
Seeking the Divine without delay.

Marvellous progress I have made,
Yes, my destiny I have paved.

Thus my loving thought energies
Hard and fast in a sneeze, bring
Overflow of happiness to seize,
Untold wealth to please,
Gracefully coming like a breeze.
Harmonious life at ease,
To be cheerful and pure as a dove,
Sagaciously sending out universal love.

I am on the look out for a

New way of thinking to be found,
Eliminating any fear,
Vowing it never again will appear, only
Earthly peace and harmony,
Radiance with certainty.

Fervently my thoughts I refine,
Ever so to define my
Affection for the Divine,
Ray of hope to shine.

Mental projection of thoughts on my mind,
Yes, what I desire I chime,

Truth to find, it's not a crime.
Hearty thoughts to align
Overall along the line,
Universally with time,
Glorious Divine order to find.
Harmony all the way by twilight,
Tenderly all through until daylight,
Serenity in all its might.

Alertness dominates within.
Remarkable! Sounds like a violin.
Ever so, I have been so keen

In getting myself into gear,
Necessary to renounce the fear.

Goodness me! I am steaming ahead,
Episodes of nullifying thoughts in my head,
Adamant for fear to disappear and
Radiance lovingly to appear.

Thinking never stops.
Harmful thoughts occasionally drop.
Off I go and take a note to
Understand how the thoughts work. I
Guarantee it makes me stop
Hence, whatever I am thinking, in a blink,
To farewell those unwanted ones, only my
Selection of thoughts in my mind to dance.

Acquire I do the habit to know that
Rampant thoughts are dangerous to let flow.
Eventually there might be ill faith, like a yo-yo. I

Use my thoughts to praise and pray,
Nothing else but the best each day.
Love universal freely I send away,
In no time, great feelings underway,
Moments to cherish and spiritually grow.
Innocence comes to the fore,
Truth is known galore,
Earnest well wishes I expect are
Due to follow and make it perfect.

The best of me is to be
Holy, that is the key.
Odd it might sound, but there it is,
Unabated coming to me,
Gently knocking, bringing harmony.
Heavenly. Dandy as candy.
Trust in the Divine I uphold,
Sounds like a pot of gold,

Happy I am to know,
Apparent it is so,
Vehement, loving thoughts to flow,
Essential for the spirit to glow.

Next, my loving thoughts go
Over the rainbow.

Bountifully, they continue indefinitely,
On their way appropriately,
Until they reach the target.
Nevertheless they come back, I do not forget,
Dare to say I am fortunate,
Awareness I have about my thoughts, I
Raise my consciousness and take notes,
Impressive all the more,
Every moment I get what I give,
Serenity, peace and harmony in my core.

There is love and care within
Heart and soul ongoing,
Out my thoughts go,
Unfailingly, they reach the goal.
Guaranteed! For I know,
Hearty energies sent fervently –
They'll come back to me silently,
Sufficient to feel the joy and harmony.

All my good deeds,
Needless to say, are my needs.
Divine soul certainly exceeds.

Warmth fills my body at once,
Obvious it becomes at a glance, if
Residue of poisonous thoughts and words
Demand a remedy, from here forward,
Surrendering to love is the reward.

Accepting the truth by becoming aware,
Reminder that thoughts and word are weapons,
Even so, they can hurt, or soothe and heal.

Well and truly, I
Evoke words to soothe and heal instead,
Always forgive, pray and bless,
Purity in my heart at best,
Obedience to myself and the Divine,
Now and forever, light to find, and
Sacred heart to realign.

Thoughts are sparks of energy,
Hard and fast they spread like a sneeze,
Onward, floating on a breeze,
Up and away, reaching the target with ease.
Gallop back, they do, and if negative,
Havoc they cause, and unrest,
Tragic events might manifest, a
Set of things less desired will beset.

Acquiring a habit of positive thinking
Readily offsets and bestows an inkling,
Each day to bring an abundance of everything.

Energising power within, fervently
Neutralising the negative apparent.
Essential to retrain the brain to acquire,
Rightfully, a fresh start to inspire,
Gracefully to be on guard, and desire
Incredible transformation to be on fire,
Extraordinary pleasant events impressed
Shaping my life as I request.

Thoughts are faster than light.
Harmonious thoughts bring delight,
Obvious, but it might not be overnight,
Until I embrace it with all my might.
Gratitude shown through a prayer.
Honestly, I will swear
To create joy instead of despair,
Sufficient for me to prepare.

Truth to know galore, I
Rejoice and let it flow,
At long last I am in harmony.
Vibrant love certainly,
Everlasting peace and health is
Likely to attract wealth.

Fair to say it's my choice
As to whether I live or perish. By
Surrendering to love I have grown,
Thus harvesting what I have sown.

Tenacious I am and alert,
Harmonious thought to assert,
Excellent flow without effort.

Perfect way to acquire,
Elation to transpire,
Another day for me to admire,
Calm and serene I infuse
Every day without excuse.

Loyal I am, it is apparent,
Outright competent,
Vivaciously brilliant,
Infinitely adamant,
Nifty and pleasant,
Generous and ardent.

Cute little child indeed,
Hopeful and sincere,
Image of the Holy at my best,
Love aplenty with zest
Delightfully I express.

I have been given a life.

Amazingly, one to be precise,
Manifesting a will to survive.

At ease on the count of five,
Longing for inner wisdom to guide to
Infinite union with the Divine,
Vigorously as I could,
Exalting as high as I should.

Blessed I am to feel free,
Overjoyed to know harmony,
Ray of hope upon me,
Nevertheless I know my boundaries.

Forgiveness is a daily plea, a
Ritual I have like a humming bee.
Effortless chore, I do it cheerfully
Each day, and embrace it gleefully.

Sure as the dawn,
Universal love I have shown,
Core of my life,
Calmly I contrive
Each day with zest
Safety to manifest,
Serenity and prosperity next.

Rejoice I do, Love Divine is on the way,
Embracing it every day,
Instantly harmonising without delay.
Goodness and success provided with speed,
Night or day, whenever the need, in a
Saintly way indeed.

Saturation in every domain,
Unseen success to reign,
Passion of mine to abstain,
Rejuvenation to maintain,
Effort worthwhile to pursue,
Many good deeds in view,
Endless wealth through and through.

Odd it might sound, but
Undeniable, I stand my ground,
Ready to be crowned.

Today and every day I rebound,
Happily I go around,
Over and above to soothe,
Unswayed, Soul Divine, as I could,
Gentle and caring as I should, without
Hesitation, loving thoughts galore,
Topsy-turvy to overthrow
Serenity to bestow.

Constant peace to know
Radiance to flow,
Ever so.
Another day within my domain,
Transformation without delay,
Endless positive thought energies on display.

Worst of all, negative thoughts
Always create knots,
Round and round, creating distress within,

Over and over herein,
Regression sure to begin.

Pay attention I do,
Eliminating doubt is a clue,
Awareness of my thoughts too, to be
Complacent is not in view,
Essential for a breakthrough.

War or peace is up to me,
Indeed if I want harmony,
Tranquil as can be,
Honesty shown freely,
Inevitable for my clarity,
Now and forever, peace within bountifully.

Lost I was once,
Oblivious to say the least.
Various thoughts I let flow,
In no time torment within did follow.
Nightly I prayed and asked why?
Grudging and complaining like a naughty child.

The answer was truth to be known, and
Honesty shown, an
Obligation to myself and the Divine,
Understanding the thought energy and the sublime,
Goodness in my heart and all hearts.
Hearty thoughts to start,
Trouble to depart,
Shine in earnest, holiness is a must.

Although change does not always come fast,
Nevertheless, when it comes it's like a blast,
Discovering the power of trust.

Warmth and kindness on display,
Onward only, without delay,
Ray of hope here to stay,
Daily prayers and well wishing underway,
Sent to the world every day.

Chain reaction roars,
Amazingly so,
Nonstop to glow.

Divine order to follow
Over the rainbow.

Wonders will never cease.
Overnight, plenty of energies
Nurture body and soul, please. I
Delight in my true self found,
Evidence that I rebound,
Ready to move forward, it is clear,
So long without any fear.

God grant me Thy wisdom, I am an
Obedient child in your kingdom, to
Demystify mysticism, about the
Splendour of your symbolism.

Legendary you are, at best.
Overjoyed I am to assist,
Vehemently I promise,
Eternally, evil to resist.

Instantly I declare my
Solemn promise with a prayer.

Unfolding love eternal with care,
Necessary for the soul to thrive without scare.
Luminous you are, and kind,
Indeed in every way Divine.
Merciful you are I know,
Innocent to the core.
Today and every day for sure,
Everlasting love will flow,
Divinity comes through with a glow.

Grandeur is in God's love,
Over and above, pure as a dove,
Divinely illuminating the path of my destiny.

Innermost body and soul embrace heartily,
Simple as that, not a fantasy.

Maintaining faith in the Divine,
Yes, I endeavour to be kind,

Learning to trust the invisible sign,
Innate strength to align.
Gentleness on my mind,
Holiness to find, is
The aspiration of my life.

Hallowed be Thy name,
Our Father in His domain, my
Loyalty is not in vain.
Integrity shown without complaint.
Nurturing the spirit within comes first,
Enables me evil to resist,
Sagaciously I exist,
Saintly as possible I persist.

I have come to believe it is
Sheer pleasure to forgive.

Meanwhile I endeavour to conceive and
Yearn for holiness to achieve.

Wisdom within bounty,
Affectionate and free, a
Youthful body and soul in harmony.

Lifelong commitment to domineer and
Old ways of thinking to disappear.
Veraciously, within my domain,
Infinitely loving thoughts to reign,
Necessary peace to gain,
Garnish for body and brain.

Temptation of evil thoughts I defy,
Happily nullified thereby,
Once and for all, never to appear again.
Unfolding inner self within my domain,
Generating powerful force to reign.
Holiness I seek, I confess,
Thankfully hoping to manifest
Success in every aspect I expect.

Indeed it's a delight.

Confident I am it will ignite,
As I am blessed downright.
Reassuring I am on target
Energising like a magnet,
Soaring high within,
Sagaciously, I thrive indefinite.

I like the thought of forgiveness, it

Paves my way to holiness,
Reaching for the sky,
Aiming to clarify.
Impression of the holy to uphold,
Simple as that, and to unfold,
Emerging a Divine Child to behold.

Prayers are powerful energies, I
Release them without question.
Aiming to project awareness, while
Yearning for Divine protection.

Attentiveness within is precious,
Now and forever strengthens and
Delightfully sends away affections,

Blessing the world every day tirelessly,
Love Divine is not a mystery, but an
Expression of my inner self entirely.
Surrounding myself with love purposefully,
Somehow life flows perfectly.

Heavenly, the Divine in you and me,
Ever creates peace and harmony, or
Acceleration of war and calamity.
Recognise what it is going to be,
The ultimate outcome – Soul Divine within?
Yearn for loving thoughts to begin.

The choice is yours and mine, whether we
Have an enjoyable time.
Our loving thoughts and words
Unfailingly make a world of difference.
Gently steer ahead and make progress, or
Hesitate and you will perpetuate, in
Time already long gone, and
Somehow, the pain will prolong

Entirely, unless our thoughts are
Very much in the here and now,
Expressing unconditional love, hope and faith, and
Repenting, it is never too late.

Might as well bless, show gratitude and forgive.
Outstanding way to receive, you'd better believe,
Remarkably wise inspiration and thought selection,
End result is abundance and elation.

Sheer joy is to do what I love, it's a
Thrilling sensation, my friend dove,
Energising and restoring every day,
Fascinating, I dare say
Kind and gentle in every way,
Affectionate like a sunshine ray.

Heavenly, I walk the path of destiny,
Appropriate with how I feel within,
Reflecting my loving thoughts.
Peaceful nature with loving words.

Almost an Angel, serene and brave,
Unfailing every day,
Talent I display,
Hearty message to convey. An
Obligation to myself and the Divine,
Rain or shine, I endeavour to be kind.

Beaming with joy, hope, love and trust,
Living life in the now, not in the past,
Exceeding my expectations fast.
Sense of wellbeing comes at once,
Sheer joy, without fuss.
Evidently I am blessed, therefore, a
Desire to continue I have for sure.

I embrace it ardently, it

Affects me instantly,
Magnifying the goodness in me.

About the author

Stefka was born during World War II in a small village tucked away in the foothills of a big mountain in Eastern Macedonia.

Her family, like others in the village, gained their food from the land. It was a self-sufficient household. This lifestyle built much confidence in her and her siblings.

She migrated to Australia in 1972, where she still resides. She finished her degree, and a diploma in counselling, and gained jobs in the welfare sector.

The last seven years before she retired were spent supporting those who experienced domestic violence. While working with people, she used her knowledge of the power of thought as a creator of our destiny. She has seen astonishing improvements when people change their attitude and implement positive and loving thoughts. Prayer, forgiveness, hope and faith go hand in hand with positive growth and attitudes.

Academic achievements

Diploma of Community Services Management

Southbank Institute of TAFE 2006

Diploma in Counselling

Australian Institute of Counsellors 1993–1994

Bachelor of Arts Degree (Major Psychology)

University of Queensland 1989

Economics, book keeping & accounting

Business Studies College (Macedonia)